Riddle Me This!

Underwater Riddles

Lisa Regan

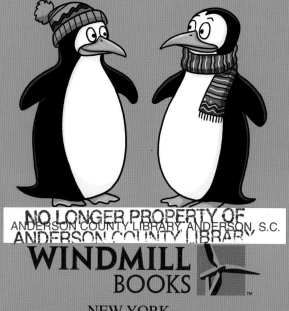

WINDMILL BOOKS™

NEW YORK

Published in 2015 by Windmill Books, An
Imprint of Rosen Publishing, 29 East 21st
Street, New York, NY 10010

Copyright © Arcturus Holdings Ltd.

First Edition

Text: Lisa Regan

Illustrations: Moreno Chiacchiera
 (Beehive Illustration)

Design: Notion Design

Editor: Joe Harris

Assistant editor: Frances Evans

US editor: Joshua Shadowens

Regan, Lisa, 1971-
 Underwater riddles / by Lisa Regan. —
First edition.
    pages cm — (Riddle me this!)
Includes index.
ISBN 978-1-4777-9177-6 (library binding)
— ISBN 978-1-4777-9178-3 (pbk.) —
ISBN 978-1-4777-9179-0 (6-pack)
1. Riddles, Juvenile. 2. Ocean—Humor. I.
Title.
PN6371.5.R47 2015
398.6—dc23

                              2013048395

Printed in the United States
SL003660US

CPSIA Compliance Information: Batch
#AS4102WM: For Further Information
contact Windmill Books, New York, New
York at 1-866-478-0556

Contents

1 If a fisherman brings home 20 buckets of fish, and his father brings home 40 buckets, who has the most fish?

2 What never gets any wetter, no matter how hard it rains?

3 What happens when you throw a white shell into the Red Sea?

Answers on page 28

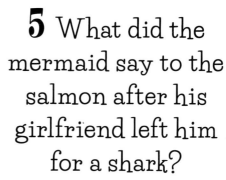

4 What am I? If you can hear where I come from, I am no longer there ...

5 What did the mermaid say to the salmon after his girlfriend left him for a shark?

6 What is found on land and at sea, although it can't be seen from either; it can be harnessed but not held, and it has no mouth, but it can be heard?

5

7 Which letter of the alphabet has the most water?

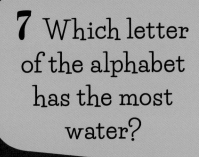

8 What kind of house weighs the least?

9 Four men were on a fishing trip. A storm blew up and capsized their boat, throwing all of them into the ocean. When they were rescued, every single man was still dry. Why is that?

6

10 Mystery Word

EACH LINE OF THIS PUZZLE IS A CLUE TO A LETTER.
CAN YOU DISCOVER THE HIDDEN WORD?

My first is in ran but isn't in far,
My second's in sea but isn't in star.
My third is in scallop and porpoise
and pearl.
My fourth's in typhoon, in twist,
and in twirl.
My fifth's in kahuna and also outside,
My first now comes back again, just
like the tide.
My last is in water and ocean
and home.
My whole is a god from mythical Rome.

11 How is the letter "t" like
an island?

7

Answers on page 28

12 What phrase is written here?
CCCCCCC

13 What's the difference between an iceberg and a clothes brush?

14 A man keeps a speedboat moored in the marina. The boat's ladder hangs over the side, and at low tide, the bottom rung just touches the water. The rungs are a foot (30 cm) apart. How many rungs will be underwater when the tide rises by 3 feet (1 m)?

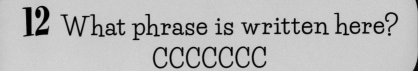

Answers on page 28

15 A ship's crew is caught in a tropical storm. They all take shelter apart from Captain Crick. He braves the elements and the lashing rain. He has no raincoat, no hat, and no umbrella. His clothes are totally soaked, rain drips from the end of his nose, and yet not a hair on his head gets wet. How can this be?

16 What is the strongest creature in the sea?

17 Which single word can be added to all these other words to make well-known phrases?
Mexican ... Micro ...
Ocean ...   Radio ...

9

18 Imagine you are deep-sea diving. You come face to face with a great white shark. You're terrified! What should you do?

19 What sea creature can swim as fast as it likes, but it never gets away from home?

20 What kind of horse do fish ride?

Answers on page 29

21 I have a beak but not a tail.
I swim around but am not a whale.
My legs are long, but I can't walk.
My brain is large, but I can't talk.
What am I?

22 Why are sea creatures with shells not fun to be with?

23 What runs into the ocean but stays in its bed the whole time?

24 Two dolphins are playing in the ocean. Dolphin A is behind dolphin B—but dolphin B is behind dolphin A. How can that be?

25 I am strong enough to walk on and heavy enough to crush roofs. But just a little sunlight will make me vanish! What am I?

26 What can be found in the middle of an ocean, that can't be found in the Atlantic or the Pacific?

Answers on page 29

27 Mystery Word

EACH LINE OF THIS PUZZLE IS A CLUE TO A
LETTER. CAN YOU DISCOVER THE HIDDEN WORD?

My first is in cottonwood, in
cedar, and in beech,
My second's in banana and also
in peach.
My third is in launch and rowing
and motion.
My fourth is in swordfish as well as
in ocean.
My fifth is in source and also in end,
My whole is a boat you can use
with a friend.

28 What has five eyes and
runs through the USA?

13

Answers on page 29

29 What happened to the pianist who worked on a cruise ship?

30 What kind of tree can you carry in your hand?

31 Two cruise ships are crossing the Atlantic Ocean. The blue ship leaves Great Britain on Tuesday. The red ship leaves the United States on Thursday but is traveling twice as fast. Which ship will be closer to the USA when they pass one another?

14

Answers on page 29

32 A zoologist is walking through a jungle and finds something in her pants pocket. It has a tail and a head but no legs. How does she know it's not dangerous?

33 An explorer is paddling up a river, when he comes to a place where it splits two ways. One way leads to a city of gold ... and the other way leads to a waterfall! He has two guides traveling with him. One guide can only tell the truth, and the other always lies. But he doesn't know which is which. What question should the explorer ask to make sure he takes the right route?

15

Answers on page 29

34 A man goes scuba diving and comes face to face with a tiger. Last year while diving, he met a bull. How can this be?

35 Dave doesn't dare go deep-sea diving in Dominica every year. Can you spell all that without any "d"s?

36 What is the number one use of shark skin in the world?

16

Answers on page 30

37 Two pirates are standing on opposite sides of a ship. One looks west and the other east— yet, they can see each other clearly. How is that?

38 What comes down but never goes up?

39 Elephants have two, but I have only one; Flippers are my arms, legs I have none. Although I'm a mammal, on land I'm never found; I live where it's coldest, the whole year round. What am I?

17

40 Can you find the name of a sea creature hidden within each of these sentences? The first one has been done for you:

(A) She wanted to wear her new tuTU, NAturally.

(B) Is that tiara yours, or did you borrow it?

(C) In case of fire, don't panic or alarm the horses.

(D) He built a lavish ark in the yard for them to play on.

41 I'm the part of the bird that's not in the sky. I can surf over the ocean but always stay dry. What am I?

Answers on page 30

42 Where does a fish keep its money?

43 Mystery Word

EACH LINE OF THIS PUZZLE IS A CLUE TO A LETTER. CAN YOU DISCOVER THE HIDDEN WORD?

My first is in swim and wetsuit
and splash,
My second's in hush but isn't in
crash.
My third is in ride but isn't in dive,
My next is in four and also in five.
My fifth is in breaker, in tide, and
in wave,
My sixth is in fright and
also in brave.
My whole is a dude who
hangs out with a board,
Perfecting a skill that is
widely adored.

19

Answers on page 30

44 If a cruise ship sinks halfway between Australia and New Zealand, in which country would they bury the survivors?

45 What won't break if you throw it off the roof of the highest building in the world, but will fall apart if you drop it into the ocean?

46 Redbeard the pirate is boasting about his many wives. "All of them are redheads, except two. All are blondes, except two. And all are brunettes, except two." How many wives does he actually have?

20

47 When Stuart goes to beach, he does something fun. When written down, this word looks the same the right way up and upside down. He ...

48 Rough and gray as rock, I'm plain as plain can be. But hidden deep inside, there's great beauty in me. What am I?

49 How can you turn a book into a stream?

21

Answers on page 31

50 There are two penguins in front of two other penguins. There are two penguins behind two other penguins. There are two penguins in between two penguins. How many penguins are there?

51 What can build castles, break down mountains, make some blind, and help others to see?

52 What did the ocean say to the beach?

22

Answers on page 31

53 A word of eight letters, found on the sea floor.
To help with your guesses, I'll tell you some more.
My first half guides sailors back home in the dark;
My second half makes a nice meal for a shark!

54 What kind of rocks are found in the Nile River?

55 What runs from front to back on one side of a ship, and from back to front on the other side?

23

Answers on page 31

Underwater Riddles

56 Mystery Word

EACH LINE OF THIS PUZZLE IS A CLUE TO A LETTER.
CAN YOU DISCOVER THE HIDDEN WORD?

My first is in turtle but isn't in liter,

My second's in yard and also in meter.

My third is in haddock and mackerel
and perch,

My fourth is in hunt and also
in search.

My fifth is in seaside and pier but isn't
in sea,

My last is in nail and also in knee.

I look like a plant, but on closer
inspection,

You'll see I'm an animal,
with spines for protection.

57 What kind of hair do surfers have?

24

Answers on page 31

58 Did you know that you can spell fish as "ghoti?" Why is that?

59 Why is it easy to weigh fish?

60 Sailors throw it away when they need to use it, but they take it around with them when they're done with it. What is it?

25

Take a deep breath, then see how fast you can say these tongue-twisters!

Six slippery snailfish slid slowly seaward.

She saw a fish on the seashore, and I'm sure the fish she saw was a sawfish.

She sells seashells on the seashore.
If she sells seashells on the seashore,
Where are the shells she sells?

Fresh fried fish,
fish fresh fried,
fried fish fresh,
fish fried fresh.

Singing Sammy seal sings songs on sinking sand.

Toy boat toy boat toy boat.

If a sailor asks a sailor,
"Say, what can you see?"
Can a sailor say to a sailor,
"Sea's what I can see!"

Eleven eels licked eleven little licorice lollipops.

Any noise annoys an oyster, but an annoying noise annoys an oyster more.

Page 4

1 The fisherman—if his father's buckets are empty.
2 The ocean.
3 It makes a splash. (Of course, it doesn't turn pink! Don't be silly ...)

Page 5

4 A seashell. If you can hear the sound of the ocean by holding it to your ear, the shell is no longer in the ocean.
5 Don't worry—there are plenty more fish in the sea.
6 The wind.

Page 6

7 The "c."
8 A lighthouse.
9 All four men were married—so no "single" men were there to get wet!

Page 7

10 Neptune.
11 It's in the middle of water.

Page 8

12 The seven seas.
13 One crushes boats, and the other brushes coats!
14 None—the boat and the ladder will rise with the tide.

Page 9

15 He is bald.
16 A mussel.
17 Wave.

Page 10
18 Stop imagining!
19 A turtle.
20 A seahorse.

Page 11
21 An octopus.
22 They are so crabby!
23 A river.

Page 12
24 They have their backs to each other.
25 Ice.
26 The letter "e."

Page 13
27 Canoe.
28 The Mississippi River.

Page 14
29 She got middle-C-sickness.
30 A palm tree.
31 When the two ships meet, they will both be exactly the same distance from the United States.

Page 15
32 It's a coin she put there yesterday.
33 He should ask one guide, "Which way would the other guide tell me to go?"—and then take the opposite route. Here's why: The guide who tells the truth will honestly tell the explorer that the liar will tell him the wrong way. The guide who lies will tell the explorer a fib about the honest man's answer. Either way, the explorer needs to do the opposite of what he is told.

Page 16

34 They are both types of shark.

35 Yes—"all that"!

36 Covering sharks, of course!

Page 17

37 The pirates are facing inward, not outward.

38 Rain, hail, or snow.

39 A narwhal (which has a single tusk instead of two, like an elephant).

Page 18

40 RAY: Is that tia**ra y**ours, or did you borrow it?

CORAL: In case of fire, don't pani**c or al**arm the horses.

SHARK: He built a lavi**sh ark** in the yard for them to play on.

41 The bird's shadow.

Page 19

42 In the riverbank!

43 Surfer.

Page 20

44 Neither—you don't bury survivors!

45 A tissue.

46 Three—one redhead, one blonde, and one brunette.

Page 21

47 SWIMS

48 An oyster with a pearl inside.

49 Add the letter "r"—brook.

Page 22

50 Four.

51 Sand. You can make sand castles on the beach; sand carried by wind or waves can erode a mountain over time; you won't be able to see if you get sand in your eyes; glass is made out of sand.

52 Nothing—it just waved!

Page 23

53 Starfish.

54 Wet ones.

55 The ship's name.

Page 24

56 Urchin.

57 Wavy!

Page 25

58 The "gh" is pronounced as in the word "rough"; the "o" as in "women," and the "ti" as in "station."

59 Because they have their own scales.

60 An anchor.

Glossary

breaker (BRAY-kuhr) A wave that breaks into foam when it hits the seashore.

capsize (KAP-syz) To be turned over in the water.

cottonwood (KO-tun-wuhd) A North American tree that produces seeds covered in white hairs.

erode (ih-ROHD) To gradually wear away earth or rock (by waves, wind, or ice).

kahuna (kah-HOON-ah) A Hawaiian word that means "magician" or "expert." The best surfer on the beach is often called the "big kahuna."

marina (mah-REE-nah) A specially designed harbor where boats are kept.

perch (PURCH) A type of large freshwater fish.

Further Reading

Dahl, Michael. *The Everything Kids' Giant Book of Jokes, Riddles, and Brain Teasers.* Avon, MA: Adams Media Corp., 2010.

National Geographic Kids. *Just Joking: 300 Hilarious Jokes, Tricky Tongue Twisters, and Ridiculous Riddles.* Des Moines, IA: National Geographic, 2012.

Websites

For web resources related to the subject of this book, go to: www. windmillbooks.com/weblinks and select this book's title.

Index